LANCASHIRE LAUGHT

Snapshots from an Atherton lad
by

Dave Dutton

Lancashire poems and stories from the author of Lanky Spoken Here and Lanky Panky.

This book is dedicated to the memory of my Grandfather, Herbert Dutton of Atherton - a Lancashire miner and soldier of the First World War.

I wish I'd known him.

CONTENTS

INTRODUCTION 3
OWD THRUMBLE'S OWD THROMBOOAN 6
IN MEMORY O' GRAN...9
CLOSURES 10
IN EAWR TEAWN.. 11
1955- 1995..12
SEAWND O'T SEA 14
NO CAROLS THIS CHRISTMAS 16
SOME ATHERTON CHARACTERS..18
THE MAD MAJOR 20
TOMMY ROACH 21
T'CUCKOO MON...23
JOHNNY ORSI..24
THE PEIGH NORRIS JOKE..25
BRICKFIELD AND THE WAKES 26
EAWR BERTHA!...30
IN AN ATHERTON WALK 32
BIRTH OF A PLASTIC PUB..35
AN ATHERTON A TO Z...36
FOR A DOOMED FACTORY CHIMNEY. 38
SURREAWNDED BI FLOWERS 40
WRONG SIDE O'T PENNINES...42
UP MARKET STREET 44
THE LANKYSHER ASTRONAUT! 47
FLOWER OF LANCASHIRE..49
A LETTER FROM THE GREAT WAR... 50
MABEL'S STORY 52
IN THE SPRINGTIME WE ROAMED BI' THE RIBBLE...............55
THE PICTURES 57
SATURDAY COWBOYS...58
ATHERTON - A BRIEF HISTORY 60
BENT - A DERIVATION?..68
DAVE DUTTON 69

INTRODUCTION

In this collection of poems, memories and stories, Lancashire actor and author Dave Dutton explores both sides of his home county: from the funny to the sad.

The grief evoked by the Pretoria pit disaster at Christmas is counterbalanced by the hilarious poem about the stunned Lancashire couple who inadvertently gave birth to a Yorkshireman!

A doomed factory chimney seems to take on a life of its own; a seaside shell evokes memories of a far away war; a family man looks back fondly at the memory of his gran; the changes in a cobbled street reflects the changes in children.

This is contrasted with the rich jumble of Lancashire life and characters like Owd Thrumble and his Trombone; Billy Milk and the Cuckoo Mon; the Saturday Cowboys - and what happens when the awful Bertha and her family pay an unexpected visit during an episode of Coronation Street. Sometimes, you'll fall about laughing. Other times, you'll be choking back the tears.

This is the first anthology by Dave Dutton, the author of Lanky Spoken Here and Completely Lanky.

It is a book you will treasure for years to come.

Oh and by the way. Did you know that according to this book, the first man in Space wasn't a Russian? It was Albert Clegg from Lancashire. Honest.

Dave: I can't pretend Lancashire is the same place it was when I was a boy growing up in the 50's. Neither is Atherton - the town I grew up in.

I hate harping back to the past but sometimes we *have* to in order to see where we are going.Even if you leave your rose-coloured spectacles on the mantelpiece, you can still see that there is a harder edge to society today.Yes the past *is* a different country. From the old pits and cotton mills came a camaraderie. Workmates were quite often neighbours. I knew the names of every person who lived in our street - and most of those who lived round the corner as well. We all went on charra trips to the seaside together. On Summer evenings all the kids played together while the grown-ups nattered on the doorsteps. Telly killed all that. Aye, things have changed but then again they always do. Thankfully though, some things remain the same.

I was born in Atherton. There is still a discernible dialect in Bent (for the benefit of furriners, that's what Athertonians call Atherton) and in Lancashire in general. There is something very comforting about hearing your own dialect spoken. It becomes a part of you. Speech patterns and words that go back hundreds of years. Words from Scandinavia and Germany. I have a website dedicated to Lancashire dialect which attracts people from all over the world. A Belgian wrote to me in wonder that we in Lancashire say hast and dust for have you and do you. *It meant exactly the same as in his native dialect in Limburg!* He couldn't understand what we had against Yorkshire folk though...

I was in an art gallery Copenhagen a few years ago and I was admiring a self-portrait oil-painting by a famous Danish artist. I remarked to the gallery proprietor that the artist looked like he enjoyed a drink. "Yes", he replied, pointing to his head. "The next morning his head always warch." (He'd got yedwarch - a headache!) I was in ecstasy - the Norwegians were actually using Atherton\Lanky dialect!

That's the romance of the dialect. That's why I have enjoyed writing these poems. A poem is merely a thought set to a rhythm and a rhyme. An observation. A snapshot. The following poems are snapshots of my Lancashire life and times. Note the word Lancashire...The bureaucrats would have us believe that Atherton is part of Greater Manchester.

You ask an old Athertonian whether he or she is a Greater Mancunian or a Lancastrian and you'll soon find out. They are Bent - and proud of it! (I hasten to point out again that Bent is the town's nickname). I hope you enjoy my words. I hope they make you laugh. I hope they make you skrike. I hope they make you think.

So turn't telly off Mother; make a brew; get yer feet up and forget about winnin't National Lottery...

'Cos you won it when you were born in Lancashire...

OWD THRUMBLE'S OWD THROMBOOAN

(Trombone).

(Winner of the Lancashire Dialect Society Poetry Competition)

Brass bands are a great feature of Lancashire life. In their own way, they contribute so much to the culture and the atmosphere of a town. On a walking day, when the churches, chapels and sunday schools parade, the first you know that the "scholars" are approaching is when you hear the strains of the band in the distance. The crowd ready themselves for the procession. Then you see the banners above the heads of the spectators floating in the air like the sails of a galleon... Mind you, you can't help laughing when it's a windy day and the banner carriers struggle to keep their feet.

But it's the band seems to set everything up just right.

This poem was loosely based on a gentleman called Bert who played in a brass band and lived at the end of our terraced row. Poetic licence has been taken with the facts.

There's an owd mon lives at th'eend o't street
We know as just "Owd Thrumble"
He's a mon who dun't ameawnt ter much
In fact he's nobbut 'umble.

Yer wouldn't turn yer yed fert gawp
If yer walked past him in't lone.
But the thing as folks all know him fer
Is Owd Thrumble's owd thrombooan.

Cos him and his owd insthrument
Are two peighs in a swod.
He'd rayther part wi't missis
Than part wi that, by God.

And when there's nowt on't telly
Or't weather's ooercast,
He teks his owd thrombooan eawt
And he dun't hawf lerrit brast!

His lungs is lahk two bellowses
And his lips is made o' flint.
He blows that 'ard deawnt meawthpiece
As it meks his eyebaws squint.

His faces terns blue, and his tung does too
As't blood to his yed goes rushin'
And his cheeks swell eawt lahk casebaws
Mon! He'd frikken Peter Cushin'!

Black Dyke and Brigeawse, Bessies too,
He's played wi't best of aw.
But they secks him, cos his high-notes
Meks aw't plaster faw off't waw.

Ter't Silver and Brass enthusiasts
He's known througheawt the land
And they caw 'im "Owd Titanic"-
Cos he dreawns aw't rest o't band.

When he comes fra werk, he has his tay,
Then eawt cums th'owd thrombooan,
An fer two-thri eawrs, he worries it
Lahk a bulldog wi a booan.

At hawf past eight, he pikes off pub
And staggers wom at ten
Then he gets his owd thrombooan eawt-
And lets it brast agen!

One neet, he stothert wom from't pub
Wi a booatload under't skin
E sucked instead o' blowin't thrombooan-
An 'oovered t'babby in!

His wahf leet eawt a piercin' skrike
And't neighbours yerd her sheawt
"Wist hafta send a ferret deawn
Fert get the bugger eawt!"

7

When Thrumble's tryin't practice scales,
It's lahk a donkey brayin'
An next dooer's dog jumps straight deawn't bog

And th'ens have aw stopped layin'.

Tha couldn't caw 'is music "canned",
It's rayther moor like "tinned"
It seawnds just like a helephant
What's troubled bad wi't wind.

Ah feels sorry fer 'is family-
Fer them there's no relief.
Poor budgy's awlus yedwarch-
And't tomcats gone stone deef.

His owd thrombooan's seen betther days,
It's like us aw, by gum.
It's owd an bent an has moor dents
Than a one-eyed jeighner's thumb.

An when Owd Thrumble drops off perch
An' thraycles off Up Yonder,
He'll tek 'is owd thrombooan wi him-
There's nowt o' which he's fonder...

An when't Good Lord anneawnces: "Ey!
It's Judgement Day morn morn."
Owd Thrumble's Thrombooan ull caw Last Thrump

COS IT'S LEAWDER THAN GABRIEL'S 'ORN!

IN MEMORY O' GRAN

A young man - married now and with a family- remembers his grandmother...

Ah see thi still, Sittin' theer
Quiet and gentle in't thowd armcheer.
Watchin' o'oer me wi a smile,
Fingers tappin' aw the while.
Though owd age had dimmed thi seet
Love shone eawt thi eyes so breet.

And in me memory still tha bakes
Parkin, hotpot,. Eccles Cakes,
Singin' Lily, prater pie,
Recipes from years gone by
Thi brand-new pinny full o · fleawr,
Oh wilt come back fer just one eawr?

Tha wouldn't lahk it neawadays
Cos theaw 'ad moor owd-fashiont ways.
So here among thi other posies
I lay to rest this bunch o' roses.
But better far, me poor heart speaks
To see some roses in *thy* cheeks.

Ahst av ter go, neet's drawin' in
And't childer's mekkin such a din.
It breyks mi heart. Ah wish tha'd known 'em.
Often thi photograph ah've shown em.
Often thi photograph ah've kissed.
Know this owd love; th'art sorely missed.

(This poem is dedicated to my grandmother, Mrs Frances Dutton, who was known to all the family simply as "Mother" and my wife Lynn's grandmother, Mrs Florrie Jones - both as Lancashire as they make them. And both still very much missed.)

CLOSURES

I wrote this after I heard Atherton Laburnum Mills was closing down. It's a street corner conversation between a young mill-worker and an older former spinner.

"Ast erd Joe?"
"Erd what lad?"
"Mill's shuttin deawn"
"Nay!"
"Aye, it's reet Joe. Last un in't teawn. Gone. Six there were one time when Cotton were thrivin'. Neaw there'll be noan Joe. Teawn's slowly dyin'"

"What's fert become Joe of aw't folk who went theer? Aw't doffers an' spinners whose lahvs have bin spent theer?"

"They'll bi thrown eawt lad, beawt bein' thanked fer their trouble. And they'll watch from their dole queues as't mill's torn to rubble"

"Cont say who's fert blame Joe? What went wrong?"
"Blame't folk who beigh chep shoddy clooers from Hong Kong. Then sheawt it eawt leawd lad, afoor it's forgotten. It were Lancashire taught rest o't world eaw't weighve cotton"

"What's gooin't happen Joe when th'owd mill has died?"

"They'll build semi's on't grave lad and fotch fooak from eawtside who know nowt nor care nowt fert traditions o't teawn. It means moor than lost jobs lad when they shut a mill deawn"

"It's gone aw quiet neaw Joe. Eee, th'owd teawn looks grey"
"That's cos its life's blood has bin drained aw away".
"That's strange Joe, ah swear ah heard't wind in't trees sighin'"
"Yon's noan wind in't trees lad. That's Lancashire. Dyin'"

IN EAWR TEAWN

In eawr teawn, we live on't dole
We've spun aw't cotton, we've brunt awt coal.
We've getten etten up bi a bigger teawn-
If things get any wuss, they'll hafta close the beggar deawn.

In eawr teawn, we think it's nice
Livin in't People's Paradise
To live wheer wur born is what we like
But we're towd we'st aft get on eawr bike.

In eawr teawn, we think it's great
Kids sniff glue an' stop eawt late;
Muggers deawn each. ginnel lurk,
But they ceawnt steyl eawr wages
Cos noan of us werk.

In eawr teawn, we're very close
If one gets 'flu, we aw gerra dose.
Wi' aw't kids names we are acquainted-
Cos they're sprayed aw oo'er't waws an' painted.

In eawr teawn, we aw gut Club
Them as dunt gut Club gut Pub.
Them as dunt gut Pub gut Bed-
But only them who've just geet wed.

In eawr teawn, there's sod all't do -
They've closed deawn't flicks and bowing greens too;
There's only Bingo but that's reet dull.
Ah'd kill mesel but Cemetery's full.

In eawr teawn, we spend aw day
Watchin' telly and suppin' tay;
Ah'd emigrate, but fer what it's worth
EAWR TEAWN IS FINEST PLACE ON EARTH!

1955- 1995

I used to love playing out when I was a child. You could never get us in. In those days of virtually traffic-free streets, we played Rolly 1-2-3; British Bulldog; Piggy; Sheppy Custard; Jack Jack Shine Your Light; I Draw a Snake Upon Your Back; Marps (Marbles); Jacks and Dobbers; Kick Out Ball; Tick; Three Pops In; Queenie; Finger Thumb Or Dumb; What Time Is it Mr Wolf?; and lots more until we called a truce by shouting *"Filly-loo-tin Milk!"*. I've never been able to work out what that meant but it did the trick...

We had Bogeys (the ones with wheels on) which we used to race down Millers Lane and the Top Field where Hesketh Fletcher School now stands. We'd play cricket down our back and the bails were the rings round the drainpipe. We couldn't half hit the ball straight...We had to because if it went in Owd Mother S****'s back yard, that was the last we would see of it. We could even pass a good half hour popping tar bubbles on hot Summer days. We didn't have a telly. We didn't have a computer - we just had a good time. This poem reflects the difference between then and now.

1955

Street's alahv wi childer, playin' childers' games.
Sheawts o' joy and laughter, rattle window-frames.
Whips'n'tops'n'kick-eawt cap, Hopscotch, knock'n'run
Swellin' eawt the seconds till't grown up game's begun.

Neighbours sit on' t dooerstep wi time fert ' ave a chat
Greetin' one another wi tawk o this'n'that.
Stage we play eawr lahvs on is a cobbled't street
Echoin' ter't clatter of eawr clog-shod feet.

Solid cobblestone and clog, clog on cobblestone.
Alder wood on cobble stood, giving way to noan.
There' a continuity reachin'' eawt from't past.
 Lahk those sturdy cobblestones, it is beawnd to last.

1995

Street lies quiet an' empty neaw Childer play no moor.
Shut away from childer's games behind locked front dooer.
Dull-eyed they stare in silence while a flickerin' image plays
And they're watchin' people murderdt in fifty different ways.

Angry guns are blastin' greyt big holes in New York Cops.
Is seein' people slaughtered moor fun than whips'n'tops?
Yesterday's happy childer are mams'n'dads today,
Too busy watchin't telly fert teych kids eaw fert play.

Eawtside on't cowd pavement, a dog howls at the moon.
Were eawr childhood just a dream - did we grow up too soon?
Echoes slowly dee away. Only one thing's sure.
They'n tarmacked o'er me memories. And't cobbled street's no moor...

SEAWND O'T SEA*

A veteran of the Atlantic convoys takes his young grandson on a trip to the seaside and the child's innocent gesture unlocks a nightmare. (Winner of the 1982 Lancashire Dialect Society Poetry Competition)

Row on row they come in hard.
Angry waves tup promenade;
Snarlin', smashin', spittin', strikin'-
O'erhead a seagull skrikin'.

Each wave dees upon the rocks,
Shattert in a million drops;
Diamonds of the sea so wild,
Each reflects a mon and childt.

'Uddledt gether, stayin'' waarm
Grandad keeps the lad from harm;
Salty-soaked an' flecked wi' spray,
Each views t'sea a diff'rent way.

Little boy picks up a shell
Tossed on't promenade bi't swell.
"Sithee grandad war ah've fun!"
"Aye lad, come on-it's time't go wom".

Back awom an' far from't sea,
T' childt sits on his grandad's knee.
He taks his little shell so dear
An' presses it ter't th'owd mon's ear.

"Neaw then grandad-what con't hear?"
Th'owd mon's eyes grow wide wi' fear-
An empty shell's awakkent dreams,
Fillt wi' feigher an' dead men's screams.

North Atlantic- Forty Three,
Torpedo makes its way through't sea.
White faced sailors 'owd their breath-
One heartbeat away from death.

14

A searin'' blast-then't sea's aflame
Fillt wi' men who skrike God's name,
Wi faces brunt, they choke an' gasp
Tossed lahk rag dolls in't th'ocean's grasp.

Desperate men claw one another
An' former comrades feight each other
Fer bits o' wood that float on't sea-
Fer who's fert live, an' who's fert dee.

Suddenly, a voice breyks through.
"Grandad! Grandad! What's to do?!"
It shatters neetmares in his yed
As th'hungry sea reclaims its dead.

"Nuthin's wrung lad - aw is well"
"But Grandad - what did't hear in't shell?"
"Nothin' owd love fert bother thee.
It's seawnd o't sea. Just seawnd o't sea..."

NO CAROLS THIS CHRISTMAS

On the Pretoria Pit disaster which happened on the borders of Atherton and Westhoughton, December 21st, 1910 when 333 men lost their lives. According to Dr. John Lunn, 28 were from Atherton.

We used to play on the site when we were children. The Ruckings we called it. They were the spoil heaps which still stand today overlooking a housing estate. As a child at St George's Infants I used to think that "the purple-headed mountain" we sang about in "All Things Bright and Beautiful" was the Ruckings!

We dropped bricks down a hole in the concrete which sealed off the mineshaft and counted the seconds as we listened out for it splashing into the water. Little did we know we were standing over the site of a tragedy which brought such great sadness to the area on that long-ago Christmas.

There'll be no carols this Christmas
And not for a very long time;
Christmas died this mornin'
Down the Pretoria Mine.

We gather round the pityard.;
Our heads in silence bow.
We were wives this morning.
We are widows now.

A cold wind in December
Blows from a sky of grey.
Below us lie our menfolk;
Cold as Christmas Day.

We'd made our plans together
Our Christmas we'd enjoy.
But now my bonny collier
Is a broken Christmas toy.

16

How can I face the childer?
How can I make them see?
That Christmas died this morning.
Christmas died with thee.

There'll be no toy soldiers for Tommy,
No dolls or ribbons for Jane
Without my bonny collier
I can never face Christmas again.

So think of my poor childer
No father to admire.
He died so you could gather
Around your Christmas fire.

There'll be no carols this Christmas
And not for a very long time;
Christmas died this mornin'
Down the Pretoria Mine.

SOME ATHERTON CHARACTERS.

OWD BILLY MILK

Everyone felt sorry for Billy Milk. He delivered groceries from house to house with a horse and cart in the 1950's. He had a shock of white hair and was bent double, like one of Lowry's Matchstalk Men, but even more so. His was a very hard life. The kids used to "plague" him by jumping on the back of his cart and getting free rides. Not that it went that fast. His horse looked older than he did - like a bag of bones on scaffolding.

One day, I had my roller-skates on when Billy's horse and cart turned into our street and I grabbed hold of a rail on the back. The sound of the skates on the cobbles spooked the horse and it "took boggarts" (ie. it took fright). It set off at a gallop which belied its age and condition and left me clinging to the back with my mam looking on open-mouthed and in shock. I managed to let go near the top of the street and careered to a halt into the factory wall. Needless to say, I never did it again.

Here is my tribute to Billy - and his old horse.

There were an owd mon who ah recaw a lung lung time ago,
He were owd as owd Methusalum and 'is 'air were white as snow;
From dooer ter dooer he sowd his wares, it were one long stop and start
And't kids aw cawed him Billy Milk - the mon wi' the 'orse'n'cart.

In Wintertime when darkness fell and't snowflakes they were droppin',
Then through aw't sleet in't cowd cowd street, owd Billy's 'orse come cloppin'
And from his owd ramshackle cart, owd Billy sowd his goods-
And his back it were bent two double, through carryin' sacks o' spuds.

Owd Billy's 'orse were lahk 'imsel - it were just a bag o bones.
It were one smaw step from't gluepot as it plodded ooert cobblestones.
An folk would aw poke fun at it, cos it were so owd an' slow-
An' eaw it poo'd yon 'eavy cart, no-one'll ever know.

Owd Billy and his trusty steed, they booath went 'ond i' glove.
 It were't th'only thing in't world tha sees as showed him any love.
They slept on't flooer o't stable deawn on Billy's mesther's farm
And they 'uddledt up tergether, just fert keep each other waarm.

But one neet poor owd Billy's 'orse tried fert struggle up a broo And
for his owd companion, it proved too much fert do. Its heart give eawt
and wi' a flop, the owd 'orse fell stone dead.
And Billy knelt and stroked th'owd lad and tears o' grief he shed.

Wi no-one left fert show him love, owd Billy faded fast And soon him
and his 'orse'n'cart were shadows o' the past. But they had no peace i'
this life - they were each on 'em 'ard-pressed.
And thur betther off so-wheer they are. They booath desarve a rest.

THE MAD MAJOR

The "Mad Major" was the name given to a local man who for reasons best known to himself always dressed up as a soldier. He was harmless enough and his baggy uniform provided a splash of khaki colour on the streets of the town. - especially on Remembrance Sunday when he took the salute on the Obelisk. I once saw him as far away as Blackpool.

It's Armistice Day. Thowd sowjers are marchin' Bi't time they get Cenotaph, their feet'll be warchin'
There's ceawncillors, clergy and loads of owd sweats There's scouts and girl guides and the brave Dunkirk Vets.

They're huffin and puffin but they'll get theer int th'end
But who's this we see as they come reawnd the bend?
Standing on't th'obelisk i' battered breawn boots It's "Mad Major" Tommy who's tekkin't salutes!

He's dressed aw i' khaki and officer's cap
And as aw eyes turn on him, there's no preawder chap.
His "rifle's" a feeshin'-rod fettled wi glue
But he showders it like he's just won World War Two.

And nobody says nowt or tries't move him on,
He's dooin no harm - he's an Atherton mon.
What matters it if he ne'er served in an army?
He's aw theer wi his mint balls - it's **us lot** who's barmy!

TOMMY ROACH

Tommy Roach was one of life's natural characters. A proud former Desert Rat, he always wore his army beret at a jaunty angle and could be relied upon to put a smile on your face, whether you wanted one or not!

He had been a professional magician on the stage and never left home without a trick or two in his blazer pocket.

Many's the time he could be seen up Market Street with a crowd round him laughing and gasping in amazement as he performed his favourite "disappearing fag" trick which involved it disappearing into his ear and re-appearing down his nose!

Tommy couldn't help himself making people laugh. In the front garden of his run-down terraced house, he would push old light bulbs into the soil to form rows and when some unsuspecting passer-by went past, he would draw on his pipe, nod at the garden and remark:" I see t'bulbs are coming up early this year..."

His house was something else. When he got a hole in the guttering, he put another gutter underneath it to catch the rain. A downspout finished halfway down the house.

He never dusted. He kept his food in plastic bags hanging on a clothes rack in the kitchen. When I asked why he said:"To keep it away from't mice. Mind you the beggars cawnt half jump!"

He slept downstairs and his television "remote control" was an old brush which he used to poke at the controls. For security purposes, he had a bedstead frame in his lobby and barbed wire round the windows - plugged into the mains supply.

Wherever he went, he picked up pieces of old slate which he used to take home and paint pictures of a surreal nature on them. Sometimes, he would display all the pictures at the front of his house.Once, when a neighbour who he didn't see eye to eye with, passed away, he stood at the front of his house playing "We'll Meet Again" on his accordion and waving a Union Jack as the funeral procession went past. When my son Gareth was a baby in his pram, Tommy peered inside and remarked:" Eee - he favvers his dad."

As I beamed proudly, he muttered "Still, as long as he's healthy that's aw as matters..." You had to laugh. That was how it was when Tommy was around.

We could do with a few more like Tommy Roach in Lancashire.

TOMMY ROACH

He's mekkin em laugh i' Market Street

He's little kids aw reawnd his feet.

He's pooin' a cig from eawt his ear!

He's mekkin hankies disappear!

He breetens life o' working folks

He's geet a million crackin' jokes

Neaw yer see him, neaw he's gone.

It's Tommy Roach - the Magic Mon!

T'CUCKOO MON

Whenever I ask anyone if they remember the Cuckoo Mon, they always look quizzically at me. But once I do the actions, accompanied by the "Cuckooo" shout in the poem, it stirs a memory in people who were around at the time. I remember him from the early 1960's. T'Cuckoo Mon must have been in his eighties - a round jolly-looking old feller who would stop when he saw a baby or a small child, bend over to stroke their heads before raising his walking-stick and yelling *CUCKOOO!* at them. Perhaps it was something he remembered from his childhood. I think it gave him pleasure seeing a child smile at his silly shout. Mind you, it probably frikkened a few an all.

T'Cuckoo Mon they cawed him
I never knew his name
As he shuffled aw deawn Market Street
"Cuckooing" were his game.
Fer every time he came across
A babby in a pram
He'd bend deawn wi a beaming face
Then turning to its mam
He'd slowly lift his walking stick
This funny little gent
And then he'd bawl eawt CUCKOOOOO!!
It'd echo aw reawnd Bent.
I don't know why he did it
But it allus browt a smile
To every little kiddy's face
And that made his life worthwhile.

*Since publishing this book, Tony Hunt has got in touch to tell me the Cuckoo Mon was his granddad – William Henry Hunt (1875-1966) who was a greengrocer with a horse and cart.

23

JOHNNY ORSI

Everybody over 40 in Atherton remembers Johnny Orsi. His picturesque little ice-cream van used to trundle round the streets of Atherton for what seemed generations. He must have spoken to nearly every person in the town. He served kids, watched them, grow, served their kids and their grandkids.

"Any raspberry?" he'd ask as he dolloped the cornet with his delicious ice-cream.

It was always a treat before you went on Atherton Park to call in at Orsi's just off Stanley Street for a delicious tub or a cornet. It was proper ice-cream made by people of proper Italian extraction. The Orsis had come to town many years before to dispense their particular brand of the home-made confection. I wonder how many cornets they sold in all that time? Probably near a million. Wonder what became of that van?

"Johnny Orsi's cummin mam
In his likkle ice-cream van!
Can I have a ninety nine?
Or a nuggit wafer will do fine.
Or mun I have a frozzen Jubbly
An orange lolly would be luvly.
A double cornet would be grand
But it allus melts aw deawn mi hand.
Perhaps I'll have Pendleton's Twicer.
We aw know that there's nowt that's nicer
I'll have a tub wi raspberry on..."
"Too late yer pie-can - he's just GONE!!"

THE PEIGH NORRIS JOKE

Peigh (Peter) Norris was another great Atherton character. He used to have a fishmonger's shop at the corner of Water Street and Church Street and always wore clogs in his shop. There was a scandalous joke that the kids used to say about him (if easily shocked turn away now).

"I see Peigh Norris was up in court last week"

"What for?"

"Showing his cod in't window!"

My mate John Davis (Junior) once told me that his dad - well-known character about town John Davis (Senior)- once went on holiday to the Isle of Man with Peigh Norris who was his friend. When they got in their room in the guesthouse, John turned to Peigh and said: "There's a terrible stink in here Peigh".

"Aye there is" agreed Peigh. "I think we'd best move digs"

It was only later as they were getting ready to go out that Peigh realised that being in a rush, he had travelled all the way to the Isle of Man with his old fishmonger's brat (apron) that he wore in the shop, under his coat.

BRICKFIELD AND THE WAKES

Facing the old Atherton Gasworks was the Brickfield. It was a large piece of spare land between Factory Street East and George Street.

I used to think it was called that because it was covered in stones and old bricks, but it could have been a place where, many years ago, bricks were actually made.

Despite the name, it wasn't even a field. I'm hard-pressed to remember there being a blade of grass anywhere in sight on it. A few weeds dared to poke their heads out of a pothole ...

The houses nearby were called Spring Gardens. No sign of a spring or even a garden there either but it was a close community. A friend of mine recalls that it was the archetypal "you could leave your back door open" type of place where a neighbour would come in and bank your fire up for you - having borrowed half a cup of sugar out the kitchenette at the same time...

The Brickfield itself was the place where the local kids used to play footy, piggy or cricket (hit the side of the Gas Works and you got a six).

The lads of the Hook family used to have their bonfire there - and woe betide anyone who tried to raid it. Our gang tried it once - even today my heart beats faster when I think about it. They chased us all the way home and I hid in a ginnell behind Massey's shop.

For most of the year it remained clothed in its dirty and uninspiring top coat but twice a year, something marvellous happened which transformed that drab dusty corner of Bent into our own homespun equivalent of the magic of Hollywood.

THE WAKES CAME TO ATHERTON!

If you are under 25, you have absolutely no idea what this meant to the kids of the town. In the early 50's, most of us didn't have tellies and we "made our own fun".

We enjoyed ourselves playing our games in the street such as but there was nothing to compare with the excitement that the Wakes brought to town.

Their caravans, some with shiny chrome-plated sides and containing exquisite pieces of porcelain china, would line the streets around and leading up to the Brickfield.

Underneath them would lie the chained up guard dogs, usually alsatians, which would leap out barking ferociously at you without provocation should you dare to venture too close.

The bigger lads used to tell you scary stories about the "gypsies" amongst them to the effect that if you got too close to them, they would kidnap you and take you away with them and put spots on your face!

Silcocks was the name of the main family who ran the Wakes. Their faces were well-known to the people of Atherton and I think I recall that the head of the family wore a bowler hat - unusual for those days to be seen outside of an Armistice Day parade.

Because they had been coming to the town for many years, a close link developed between them and certain Atherton families - some of the local girls even baby-sat for them.

Two of the regular Wakes men were brothers who had suffered horrific burns (it is said that they threw a match into an oil drum and it exploded in their faces.)

Excitement built and we watched in wonderment as the travelling fair gradually took shape... the Waltzer; the Noah's Ark; Chairoplanes, the Dodgems; the Big Wheel; the Whip and all the various side-stalls.

We took good care not to get in the way of the burly "wakesmon" as he would frequently let loose with a few choice epithets should this be the case.

When the wakes opened on the Friday evening, we all flocked grasping our pennies and tanners and thripenny bits which our loving parents, aunties and uncles had given us - and the world was our hot dog!

As we walked nearer and nearer, the butterflies would start as the pop music of the day (for some reason I remember Here Comes Summer) got louder and louder as we approached and the flashing coloured lights of the rides got brighter and brighter and the throb of the mighty generators with names like King Kong echoed the throbbing of our own hearts .

Then the smell of the candy floss and the fried onions got stronger and stronger...then we were there!

27

On't Wakes!

No longer the Brickfield but paradise on earth with all the glamour a junior Athertonian could handle.

The little uns would make for the small roundabouts, usually near the Mealhouse Lane end, and sit in an open-top Dragon or a small trolley bus or aeroplane and go round and round waving at mam.

The big uns would flock to the Waltzer which spun them round giddily but which sometimes had a hidden bonus.

Because of the movement of the carriage, change would often be flung out of trouser pockets to disappear down the back of the seat. Our hands would surreptitiously feel down the cracks to see what we could retrieve, taking good care not to let the wakesmon see us otherwise he might feel disposed to give us a clout, for he perceived all loose change as one of the perks of his lowly-paid vocation.

Though it was probably the tamest and most boring ride on the wakes, the Caterpillar proved popular with lads and lasses of a certain age as when the green corrugated cover came over half-way through the ride to make it look like a huge circular caterpillar and hid the people on the ride, that was when the opportunity was taken for a quick snog.

Many a flirtation - and probably a marriage or two - started on the bumpy old Caterpillar ride.

The Penny Slots were a popular place which probably started one or two Athertonians on the rocky road to Gamblers' Anonymous. They were in a large tent containing wooden shelves full of old "catchpenny" machines which are now worth a fortune as collectors' items.

On some of the machines was a disc with several colours on and you could bet on which colour would stop against the arrow.

If you look at the old Wild West films, you can usually see a similar machine in the saloon bars!

Next to the Penny Slots was Butterworth's Black Pea Saloon where "blanket-lifters" were a speciality.

Some people also called them musical fruit, for reasons which should be fairly obvious.

Pigeon peas were boiled in a large cauldron fired by coke and served in thick white cups into which a squirt of vinegar from a little pot barrel was added, if requested.

They were eaten in their own gravy with a spoon and boy did they taste good. It may have been the fumes off the coke or the rust from the cauldron that added something but try as you may, you could never get the same taste when you tried to do black peas yourself at home.

Inevitably, after trying your luck at the Blackjack and Roll-a-Penny stalls, your little stock of cash would dwindle away to nothing. You never seemed to want to go home though.

Like a magnet the wakes was...

Nowadays, the "Brickie" is no longer there. Blocks of flats stand on the spot of so many happy childhood memories. One less place for kids to play. One less place for them to enjoy themselves. But being one of the lucky ones, I can still close my eyes and see and hear and smell it all, so I'm off to the Wakes again.

In my dreams...

EAWR BERTHA!

Picture the scene. You are just settling down for the night to eat a slavvery duck and watch a bit of Coronation Street when a knock comes to the door. And it's always the relative you most fear. The one you want to avoid at all costs. The evening's ruined. In this case it's.... Eawr Bertha!

Eee, Look who it is - it's eawr Bertha...and Tommy and't childer an aw!

Eee, well ah'm reet fain fert see yer...come in, it's so nice of yer't caw.

Just when I'd finished me weshin...th'only chance I've had t'put up mi feet.

Ahst be powfagged ter death wi' her natterin - an I'll miss Coronation Street"

In't it funny, I just said ter Charlie, we ne'er see eawr Bertha and hers,

Next minute, you tern up on't dooerstep. Well. I'll gu ter the foot of eawr sturrs!"

What ah <u>said</u> were, ah bet Bertha's sulkin ooer yon sewin' machine o' me mam's.

Well she promised it me when owt happened to her. They con lump it, ah don't gi a damn!"

And look at the kids, aren't they bonny - they're a credit ter thee and Tom too.

What's that tha sez Bertha, they're brainy an aw and they're dooin' reet weel at skoo?

Well ah cawnt see as who they tek after - we've getten moor brains in eawr cat.

Cos 'er were as numb as a pit prop - and Tom's even thicker than that!

What dust say - yer've geet summat fert tell me? Eee Bertha what's up, yer've gone grey.

Yer gooin ter't th'Infirmary next Tuesday fert have everythin' tekken away?!

Well, there's nuthin new theer eawr Bertha - it's happened befoor ah'll be beawnd.

Ah thowt yer'd had everythin' tekken away last year - when't bailiffs came reawnd!

Have I heard abeawt who - Nellie Hargreaves? Her husband is gerrin' a divorce.

Cos he copped her at back o't Red Lion wi a bloke eawt o't Royal Air Force...

That's pon cawin't kettle eawr Bertha. Th'art fond o' thi own little treats.

And th'art tekkin in moor than just washin' - especially when Tommy's on neets!

What's that then? Yer've got ter be gooin'? So soon? Eee my doesn't time fly?

Yer know yer me favourite sister. Come again luv and soon mind. Bye bye...

Thank goodness they've gone. Ah can settle. Oh, Coronation Street's finished. Worra waste.

She wouldn't be so bad would eawr Bertha - if she wasn't so ruddy two-faced!

IN ATHERTON WALK

I can't claim credit for the next piece of Atherton memorabilia. It's something we've had knocking about the house for years. The anonymous writer has cleverly woven into the walk around Atherton the names of some of the pubs that were standing at the time - probably towards the early part of the century. Some still are - others are but a memory.

I particularly regret the passing of the Prince Saxe-Coburg or "Mick's" as it was better known, after Mick McCabe, a former landlord.

It was frequented by our family for years - my grandmother Mrs Frances Dutton used to enjoy a Mackeson or two there. The tap-room was brilliant - I spent part of my formative years there enjoying the company of a rich mixture of characters, quaffing Magee's Best Bitter (and sometimes if I was feeling reckless, the Indian Pale Ale) and learning the finer points of dominoes.

There were Lancashire lads, Poles, Irish, Ukrainians, miners, millworkers, undertakers, old soldiers, railwaymen in fact blokes from all walks of life, most of whom enjoyed their dominoes and took it really seriously in view of the fact that a tanner was at stake and sometimes penny a knock. And the inquests after a game - oh the inquests!

No women were allowed in - except Ethel who brought the beer. You wouldn't get away with it in these politically correct times but it was somewhere the lads could go to relax, let loose a few cuss words and generally have a ruddy good laugh and a natter without disapproving feminine glances. And where's the harm in that?

You don't seem to get the same laughs in pubs these days or the same amount of characters.

Perhaps the pool tables and the juke box has killed conversation - not to mention the price of the booze.

Here are some Atherton pub tales. They're all true - honest...

- An argument once started in the Letters Inn about who had the biggest canary. The next day, one bloke came in with a whopping great canary and claimed victory. On closer

32

inspection by the landlord, it was found to a blackbird that he'd painted yellow...

- A regular at the Rope and Anchor used to worry rats with his teeth and take bets on how long it would take him to dispatch them.
- One regular at the Bear's Paw swore that he had a tame sparrow and made a bet with the other customers who didn't believe him. He came in the next day with it on his shoulder (He'd caught the unfortunate bird and sewed its legs to the shoulders of his jacket.)
- A few years ago, there was the regular at the Spinner's Arms who used to take his bowls in a plastic bag. Someone substituted them and when he got to the bowling green, two turnips rolled out!
- The landlord of the Prince Saxe once glued a half crown piece to the floor next to the gents and the regulars used to laugh at people's attempts to pick it up or kick it through the door of the toilets.
- Bob Ellis, the brilliant former mine host at the Concert Inn, had many a pub trick to keep people amused but his best party piece was to come out dressed as the Pope blessing the astonished people at the bar! (A friend of mine who was causing a nuisance of himself was once hung up on a hook on a beam in the pub until he promised to be quiet).
- At the turn of the Century, my grandfather Sam Dutton put laxative in the beer of a brass band playing Christmas carols in the Mountain Dew causing them to stop blowing and beat a hasty retreat to the gents!

Here then is a walk round the old pubs of Bent a long long time ago. Where were they all though? (That'll cause some arguments...!)

IN AN ATHERTON WALK

As I was coming from Atherton Central Station the other day, I saw the Blue Bell deliberately plucked by the Spinners Arms. As I sat under the Oak Tree on the Traveller's Rest gazing at the Swan, I was tapped on the shoulder by the Bear's Paw which gave me to understand that I was being chased by the Red Lion.

In making for safety, I ran against the Bull's Head, where I was tossed up right above the Rising Sun but fortunately, I alighted on something soft which turned out to be the Wool Pack.

The King and Queen seeing my dangerous position, rendered first aid by giving me a sip of Mountain Dew.

In a little while came the Jolly Nailor who, with the help of the Bricklayer's Arms carried me and laid me safely behind the Wheatsheaf where I was attended by another royal friend - the Prince Saxe-Coburg who seeing that I was New Inn Atherton mixed me a bottle from the Punch Bowl and seeing that I was a stranger and a man without a name had me placed very gently on the arm of Shakespeare and taken from down Bag Lane to be laid to rest in the Ancient Shepherd's Home.

After regaining my strength, I was taken on the back of the Elephant and Castle and put on the London and North Western Railway where I resumed my journey in safety...

BIRTH OF A PLASTIC PUB

This is self-explanatory. I didn't like what the breweries were doing to the pubs in Lancashire in the 1980's (and still are to some extent). So I wrote this...

First, they tore out the original oak beams
And slapped in olde plastic facsimiles.
Then they rooted out the jovial, red-faced, shire-horse of a landlord,
And replaced him with a surly glove-puppet, with a carved-in snarl.
Then they flushed out all the good, strong, draught ale down into the sewers,
And piped in what had previously been in the sewers.
They booted out the old concertina man
And installed a head-throbbing jukebox
(To stop people talking about what was happening).
This forced out all the customers with any character
And in their place, came.....
Well; suffice it to say that one night,
A member of the new clientele stood too near a lamp

And melted.

AN ATHERTON A TO Z...

Just a little tribute to my home town. Probably yours was similar if you came from Lancashire.

A IS FOR ATHERTON - A PROPER LANKY TEAWN

B IS FOR BLACKLEDGE'S WHOSE CHIPS WERE GOLDEN BREAWN.

C'S FER CHOWBENT CHAPEL WHEER ME AND'T WIFE GEET WED

D'S FERT MUCKY DOGGY BRUK, FILLT WI DOGS WHAT'S DEAD.

E'S FER GOOD OWD EKKY FLECK WHEER'T SCHOLARS ARE SO BREET

F IS FER THE FORMBY HALL WHERE WE DANCED AW SETDY NEET.

G'S FER GREASY JOHNNY WHO BATTERED HIS FLAT CAP

H IS FER HEAW BRIDGERS WHO ALLUS LIKED A SCRAP

I 'S FER ICKY T'FIRE BOBBY. (WHO THE HELL WERE HE?)

J'S FER JACK LOWE'S CLOOERS SHOP, WI'T SHUTTLE WHIZZIN' -WHEEEEE!

K'S FER KIDDY'S KORNER WHICH WERE FULL O' BELTING TOYS

L'S FERT LITTLE HOLLOW, FULL O' SWEETS FER GIRLS AND BOYS.

M IS FER THE MAYPOLE AND'T TROLLEY BUS OUT OF TOWN

N'S FER NAILS WHICH LONG AGO MADE ATHERTON RENOWNED

O IS FER THE OBELISK AT TH'END O' MARKET STREET

P'S FERT PUNCH BOWL PETTIES WHICH ALWAYS SMELLED SO SWEET.

Q IS FER THE OWD QUEEN'S YED - A PUB OF FORMER DAYS.

R IS FER THE RUCKINS WHEER WE SLID DEAWN ON TIN TRAYS.

S IS FERT SAVOY'S BACK SEATS WHEER WE WENT FER DOUBLE TOP!

T IS FER THE TEMPERANCE BAR, TOP FIELD AND THOWD TOP SHOP.

U'S FERT UNITARIANS - AN INDEPENDENT LOT

V IS FER THE VALLEY - ONCE A PLEASANT LITTLE SPOT.

W IS FER WALKING DAY WHEN'T KIDS GO THROUGH THEIR PACES

X IS FOR THE KISSES THAT THEY AW WIPE OFF THEIR FACES.

Y GO ANY FURTHER? ME RHYME IS NEARLY SPENT

Z JUST STANDS FER ZEBRA - AND THERE'S NOAN O' THEM I' BENT!

FOR A DOOMED FACTORY CHIMNEY.

When the factory chimney belonging to Howe Bridge Mills at the corner of Mealhouse Lane and Bag Lane, was knocked down, I went to watch.

There were scores of people there including some, I imagine, who had worked at the mill and who came away more than a little heavy-hearted and sad that this familiar landmark had been taken away. It reminded us that the cotton industry which, along with the pits, had been the life-blood of the town was in decline and it was one less link with the past.

It reminded me of a public execution. So I attributed a personality to the old chimney and went home and wrote this poem in memory of it.

Creawds o' folk have come fert watch thi dee,
Owd familiar friend.
Th'art useless and unwanted dosta see.
Thi life mun end.

Preawd tha stonds like one o't th'upper crust.
Soon tha'll be gone.
And of thi memory, there'll be nowt but dust.
Like mortal mon.

For years tha played a leading part on't stage
And played it well.
And saw th-awf-timers through to ripe owd age
Just like thisel.

Whene'er tha breathed, tha breathed life into't place
But that's in't past.
When Progress says "I dunnot like thy face"
Tha's breathed thi last.

Here comes thi executioner deawnt street.
Thi life is dun wi.
I'm sure tha'd try't escape if tha'd but geet
Some legs fert run wi.

Creawds hushed and silent neaw and then comes one
Almighty crack.
Tha topples o'er and then tha's gone
Wi brokken back.

And th'eyes that watched thi faw neaw fill wi tears.
Folk realise.
Theaw were a symbol o' their workin' years.
Neaw dead tha lies.

An epitaph fer thee I've written deawn
I'll say it clear.
Here lies t'body of a forgotten cotton teawn

RIP Lancashire.

SURREAWNDED BI FLOWERS

My mum Mabel worked in Howe Bridge Mill. This is for her...

Me mam were an ordin'ry Lancashire lass-she'd worked in the mill
most her life
An' though many's bin dulled by the factory grind, mi mam she were
sharp as a knife.
She loved aw the beauties o' nature an' she'd sit in the garden fer
hours.
An' the songs o' the birds'd dreawn th' echoes o' t' looms as she sat
theer-surreawnded bi flowers.

Fer't bi shut in a factory's not natural, for aw folk need clean air an'
leet,
But when mam escaped from t' mill's greedy grasp, she'd tek us on't
moors, green an' sweet
An' we'd romp lahk young foxes in t' sunshine, revellin' in Earth's
healing powers.
An' mam'd lie dreamily dozin' on't grass. contented- surreawnded bi
flowers.

Ah remember one time, mi mam's birthday, when money were scarce
an' life 'ard,
We'd 'ardly an 'awpenny between us- we couldn't afford t' price of a
card.
So we gathered her favourite wildflowers, from t' meadows an'
hedgerows an' bowers
An' we gave 'em th' owd girl, you'd've thowt they were pearls; she sat
sobbin'- surreawnded bi flowers.

Aw them long years she worked in the factory took a toll on her health
it were plain,
An' though she had mony an illness, not once did Ah hear her
complain.
An' then when owd age kept her prisoner, in t' shadow o' t' dark
facthry towers

40

Ah knew that her heart were still out theer, in t' country-surreawnded bi flowers.

T' day that she left us were't day as Ah skriked. Ah lay a red rose on her breast,
Her owd workmates had aw clubbed together an' bowt her just what she loved best.
An' as t' cars drew away from t' front dooerstep, mi tears fell lahk warm salty showers.
Till Ah realised, she'd gone as she'd want to have gone, At rest,

Surreawnded bi flowers...

WRONG SIDE O'T PENNINES

This is a cautionary tale of a Lancashire couple who were misguided enough to take their holidays in Yorkshire. She was eight months gone an all! The last line shows though that everything is relative...

TH'USBUND:

Poosh! Poosh! Poosh Bessie lass.
One moor thrutch'll do.
Hoosh! Hoosh! Ne'er mind yon gas.
Ah think he's comin' through.

Sithee! Sithee! Eawt he pops -
A pratty babby lad!
Neaw we'st aw get drunk as mops.
Ah'm a bonny beawncin' dad!

Huch up! Hutch up! Mek room in't bed
Ah feel ah'm gooin't swoon.
Since babby took it in its yed
T'arrive three wick too soon.

Eigh up! Eigh up! Ah'm in a daze.
Worrast gone and done?
Tha's had t'babby on eawr holidays
Ninety mile from wom!

Oh eck! Oh eck! why did we pick
On Scarborough of aw places?
We met have hatched a little chick
But we've egg all ooer eawr faces...

Pass gas! Pass gas! Me pulse has gone
Dust realise? It's a shocker.
Tha's given birth to a *Yorkshiremon*
Tha must be off thi rocker!

Ay my! Ay my!.. Pass th'ankicher.
Ah think ah'm gooin't skrike.

42

Ah've a season ticket fer Lankysher
Neaw ah'm t'feyther of a TYKE!

Owd up! Owd up! This is no joke
Tha knows me dearest speawse.
Ah cawn't abide them Yorkshire fooak
Neaw we've getten one int theawse!

It's bad! It's bad! Witheawt a deawt.
Heawever will we fare?
We'll ne'er know what he's on abeawt
Cos them Yorkshire fooak tawk quare!

That's it! That's it. Ah'll affert flit
Tha shoulda gone on't Pill.
When me mam finds eawt abeawt it
Er'll cut me eawt o't will!

The shame! The shame! Ah'll ne'er go back.
Ah daresn't show me face.
Ah'll stop this side o't Pennines
And dee in deep disgrace.

T'WIFE:

Nay lad! Nay lad! Don't tek it so bad
Tha forgets one thing mi dear.
He met have bin born i' Yorksher
But he were MADE I' LANKYSHEER!!

TH'USBUND:

Tha'rt reet! Th'art reet! Ah must be thick.
Things could be worse eawr Bessie.
If we'd gone to Brighton for the wick.

HE'D HAVE BIN A SOUTHERN JESSIE!

UP MARKET STREET

Go for a walk up Market Street - or any other main Lancashire shopping street - and you can guarantee that if you've lived in the town for any length of time, it'll take you nearly an hour to walk a couple of hundred yards. That's because Lancashire folk love a good natter and Market Street is where they catch up on everything. By the time you get to the pie shop, you've forgotten what you went in for! But that's great. That's the essence of a friendly Northern town that no out-of-town supermarket can ever provide.

My mother Mabel was a familiar sight up Market Street. She used to say: "Eee - I've been stopped by ever so many folk - I didn't have time to do me shopping." She would meet old workmates, old schoolfriends, members of the family who she hadn't seen for ages and people she had only met "up Bent" (as we call going up Atherton) but who she used to go for a cup of tea and a cake with in one of the local cafes. It was an important part of her life - as was going on Atherton Market on Fridays.

I would like to thank all those who had a natter with her - especially the local shopgirls who always found time for her. It must have been like this for a few hundred years.

 Little groups of folk huddled together exchanging juicy bits of gossip and passing comments on everything from the weather to how dear things have become.

Market Street has changed. There were no shutters or spy cameras when I was a lad. But it's still a treat for people to stop and be stopped. Even when you are in a hurry for your pie... The poem doesn't scan. I did it how folk talk.

We're havin' a natter up Market Street
We're puttin the world to rights.
We talk abeawt owt - from't price o sprouts
Ter't cheapest place fer tights.

We know who's dooin' what to who
And when and where and how

And what happened next an' dearie me
There were a flamin' row!

Eee look at that wench
She favvers she's getten two caseballs up her sweater.
And in't it sad heaw things've changed
And never fer the better.

An look who's comin eawt o't pub
She looks like she's in't puddin' club
That's third un - all bi different blokes
In't it surprisin' eaw some folks
Cawnt keep their knees together.
An Nellie, what abeawt this weather?

It were ne'er like this until they started
Puttin' shukkles up in space
An look o'er theer at yon mon's face.
It favvers a bad ham - spittin' image of his mam

And her were as fow as a summons. Worra wummun.
Ne'er had two haypennies rub tergether.
Funny family. Had another son wi a lazy eye
Cawed Fred. (Funny name fer an eye!)
Wouldn't get eawt o' bed.

They feawnd him dead. Summat went in his yed.
That's what Doctor said.
Scandalous what they charge for bread. These days.
In't it?
Look at that Alsatian o'er theer! Ey thee. Stop it dooin that!
I can go and do what?! Don't be so ruddy lippy.
You cudda dragged it away from't front o't chippy.

No Cumberland sausage fer me fer mi tea.
Mucky get. Tek it vet and have it seen to.
What charm school has yon mon been to?
No consideration some fooak. Not geet no flamin' tact.
Eee I see your dowter Brenda's thin as a lath.

There's moor meat on a scabby cat.

Sez it's anorexia. I bet she's only doin' it to vex yer.
Still, she'll be cheap to keep.
I expect. Which reminds me...
Ah'll haft to go or else our Joe's dinner
Ull be brunt to a cinder

Oh dear God Almighty our Jade Elizabeth
Stop lickin' that ruddy shop winder!
It's one o' them theer Sex Shops-It's disgustin'.
They've aw sorts o' funny things in theer.
And they aw need a good dustin'!

We've never needed sex reawnd 'ere before -
Why should we need it neaw?
If Bert brings any o' them things wom
There'll be a flamin' reaw.

Ey up. I cawnt stond here aw day. I'm gettin' flamin' wetter.
Ay my, eaw things've changed reawd here.

And I wouldn't say fer the better...

THE LANKYSHER ASTRONAUT!

A lot of misguided folk will try to tell you that the first man in space was a Russian chap called Yuri Gagarin. This is a load of burnt tripe.The authorities have for many years hidden the fact that this pioneer of cosmic exploration was in fact a bloke from Atherton.

Jealous of the fact that it was a Northerner, a Lancastrian, an Athertonian and a Chowbenter to boot who beat everyone hands down, they tried to give the credit to someone else - yes, even a foreigner. The truth has not been out there.Until *now*, as I reveal for the first time that the world's first astronaut was none other than a man who built his own space rocket in a shed on his allotment down the Valley in Atherton.I am more than happy to pay tribute to this brave pioneer of outer space who boldly went where no bugger had went before with no other soul for company but a manky ferret named Joe.

This is his story. Ladies and gentlemen. Please salute MR ALBERT CLEGG...

Now Albert Clegg he had a plan to make himself a famous man:
He'd build a rocket in his shed and fly to Outer Space he said.
He welded 26 dustbins and fastened 'em with panel pins.
And he planned to explore the Galaxy, with his ferret Joe for company.

Now t'Yanks and t'Russians laughed and said he'd got a screw loose in his yed
But Albert thought he'd let 'em scoff and soon came time for blasting off
And sat on 50 tons of fuel, he tried to look all brave and cool
Then blowing kisses to his mum, he blasted off to Kingdom Come.

Who's that floating through the sky, eating plates of Tater Pie?
It's Albert Clegg the Human Fly, he's the Lankysher Astronaut..!

Our Albert floated through the stars and just for luck turned left at Mars,
But he let his ferret take control and he landed in a big Black Hole
Though rough and bumpy was the ride, he came out at the other side.
Said Albert to his ferret: "Joe, it's to the lavvy I must go"

When Albert went to spend a penny on't lavatory, there wasn't any!
Said Ferret Joe: "Tha gormless foo! Tha's forgot fer't build thiself a loo!"
Albert's tears fell like confetti. Ten light years from't nearest petty!
"Ah've done it now" said Albert Clegg. "It's tricklin' down me inside leg!"

If you look up in't sky at night, you're bound fer't see an eerie light
Forget those tales of UFO's - it's Albert and his ferret Joe
Both doomed to roam the Galaxy, looking fer a lavatory;
In hope to empty Albert's clog, they search for yon Celestial Bog.

So think of him in Outer Space with both legs crossed and red in't face.
Lankysher's first Astronaut. Spacemon and Ferret both caught short.
And next time that you're wandering round and showers come a-tumbling down.
It might not be rain from clouds what's shed. But Albert, piddling on yer yed!

- **There is a strange sequel to this story. I wrote this poem many years ago. Years later, I was up for a part on Emmerdale on Yorkshire television. The other person being considered was no less than my old friend Bernard Wrigley, alias the Bolton Bullfrog, with whom I have written many songs as well as appearing with him at many of the North West's largest theatres. The part in question was for a character named Barry CLEGG. Who was a nutcase who built a space rocket in a shed on his farm! (It eventually blew up and set fire to the place). How's that for a spooky coincidence? Bernard got the part...**

THE FLOWER OF LANCASHIRE

Dedicated to the Lancashire lads who never came back.

The Flower of Lancashire marched to war and a bugle played a sad farewell
With banners flying and women crying and who'll come home again none can tell.
Farewell to Sarah and bonny Mary - oh say goodbye to your soldier bold.
For he's only an ordinary Lancashire lad and he's only doing what he's been told.

From cotton towns to foreign downs, from coal mines dark to trenches dank.
He's changed his clogs for soldiers' togs and on to death goes rank by rank.
No more he'll hear the skylark calling him on his beloved Pennine moor.
He'll only hear the bullets sing now the King needs him to fight his war.

They plucked him from his Lancashire soil to go and fight a faceless foe.
But roses soon will fade from bloom in a place where only poppies grow.
A rifle's aiming and death is claiming him: there's no time to shed a tear.
A rose lies dying. In mud he's lying. The blood red rose of Lancashire.

*Dedicated also to my grandfather - Herbert Dutton who served in the trenches and got blown up and shot for his trouble. The poem has also been set to music and sung by my friend Bram Taylor from Leigh. It's available online..

A LETTER FROM THE GREAT WAR...

THE FOLLOWING IS A LETTER I HAVE IN MY POSSESSION FROM CPL T WHITTAKER OF BURNLEY TO HIS FRIEND AND FELLOW SOLDIER (AND MY GRANDAD) HERBERT DUTTON OF ATHERTON, WHO SERVED IN THE KING'S OWN ROYAL LANCASTER REGIMENT; THE SUFFOLK REGIMENT AND THE LINCOLNSHIRE REGIMENT. IT IS WRITTEN IN PENCIL FROM A CONVALESCENT HOSPITAL IN FRANCE AND, LIKE MEMORIES OF THOSE AWFUL TIMES, IT IS NOW FADING.

MY GRANDAD WAS AN ATHERTON MINER. HE PLAYED FOOTBALL FOR ATHERTON COLLIERIES AND THE INDEPENDENT METHODISTS AND WORKED AS A VERY YOUNG CHILD AT PRESTWICH PARKER'S SMITHY IN BAG LANE. AS A COLLIER, HE WORKED DOWN GIB, CHANTERS AND CLEWORTH. HE VOLUNTEERED AT THE AGE OF 33 YEARS TO JOIN THE ARMY AND IN DECEMBER 1914 HE BOARDED THE TRAIN AT LEIGH FOR HIS REGIMENT IN LANCASTER. HE SERVED IN FRANCE ON THE SOMME AND WAS WOUNDED TWICE AND BURIED BY A SHELL.

HE WAS DEMOBILISED FROM THE LINCOLNSHIRE REGIMENT IN JANUARY 1919 AND RECEIVED A WAR GRATUITY OF £23 LESS ONE POUND *PAYABLE ON RETURN OF HIS MILITARY GREATCOAT*.

HE WENT TO WORK DOWN THE MINES AGAIN AND DIED OF PNEUMONIA AT THE YOUNG AGE OF 53 IN 1935. THIS LETTER BRINGS HOME THE REALITY OF THAT TERRIBLE WAR AND THE CONDITIONS THESE LANCASHIRE WORKING-CLASS LADS HAD TO FACE.

Monday May 29th, 1916.

Dear Old Pal,

I now take the Pleasure in writing you a few lines as I know how you will want to know my experiences in the boxing ring. Them were the days Dutton. Well, I have been in hospital with swollen feet but it was with standing in the trenches up to the knees in water. You know 8 days is a fair while to be stood up and we never got to close our eyes all the time.

You might not believe it but it is true enough and the Germans sent their gas over and 78 were gassed and when the artillery start, they don't send shells, they send foundries over.

What a life Dutton. I could not make you believe what it is like. There was some mines blown up and believe me, I thought it was lights out and the ground trembled like a jelly.

We were only 25 yards from the German trenches, so you will understand why we had no sleep. I had a private in my sentry group. It got on his nerves to such an extent that he went stone mad. Directly after, a shell came and hit a fellow from Nelson but he was in fragments and I picked up his top lip with his tash on. So you will have an idea of what it is like here.

Harper is here and he is no friend of the men. They do not like him. Swallow is here and Wright. As regards my first coming out here we landed at a place and stayed there about a week and we were sent up the line to another place on the 2nd of April which was a Saturday and on the Sunday, we joined the battalion and at about 4-30 the O.C. came and said we had a trench and crater to take and at 6-30 we set off to our task.

When we had gone so far, we had to get our faces blackened and off we went again. At 2-10 on the Monday morning, we had got to where we had to make the bayonet charge and before I knew where I was, I had fallen into a German trench and of course, I was a bit dazed but I soon jumped up when I heard someone shout "Mercy Comrade". It was dark and I had a job to find out where the noise was coming from, so I felt with my hand on the floor and I could just feel the head of the German.

He was buried all but his head - wait for it - and then seven came walking towards me with their hands up asking for mercy but they got it. I can assure you Dutton it is no picnic going into a bayonet charge. It is not like charging sacks. Then after the charge comes the bombardment. That is worse than the charge.

Remember me to Bob Jones 42 and Sgt. Major and the Q.M., I mean Hulton. Is French with you yet?

I will draw this letter to a close with best wishes for your welfare. I will tell you what Dutton, I could do with some tackle to clean my buttons as we have to clean them when out of the trenches. So no more this time from your old pal Whit. Buck up. Write back soon Dutton as I shall not be here long. Address as follows.

Cpl T. Whittaker 16731 K.O.R.L. Regt No 1. Convalescent Camp, Boulogne.

(I wonder if Corporal Whittaker survived the War?)

MABEL'S STORY

If you think you have it hard in your job today, take a look at the following article written by my mother Mabel, an Atherton lass all her life, about her experiences during the Second World War at Risley when young girls from Atherton and Lancashire in general were made to work in the munitions factories as part of the war effort.

"I started work at Risley Royal Ordnance Factory at near Warrington when I was 19 years old. I was told I had to go to work on Group One. That group was nicknamed the Suicide Group on account of the many workers who had been blown up, killed, maimed or blinded. I didn't know it at the time but I would be working with highly explosive gunpowder for making detonators. On the first day, 12 of us from all over the place had to go into admin to be issued with a book of rules. There were three working shifts - Mornings; Afternoons and Nights.

Eleven went to Group Five Powder but I had to wait for a guide to take me to Group One.. It was then I noticed that she only had one hand and a finger missing off the other hand. I asked her what had happened and she made up some story or other. I later found out that she had had them blown off when she went to work on Group One.

I had to start on the afternoon shift which was 2 until 10 pm. I caught the bus from the Punch Bowl at Atherton to Leigh and then another bus from Union Street to Risley. Then we went on rickety wooden ones we called cattle trucks for about a mile to Group One.

Outside, we had to leave our coats, shoes, bags, money, hairclips and anything metal in the Contraband Place and change into any old worn shoes, overalls and white turbans. I had bags, money, make-up, photographs and purse stolen many times. Even my own shoes.

On my first afternoon there, I was put in the Experimental Shop where we had to test the powder by weighing them on brass scales and sealing detonators one at a time. We had to wear goggles and leather gauntlets. One day I was given a red box to carry with one person in front and behind carrying red flags walking along the clearways, taking them to be stored in magazines to be used later.

I didn't know what I was carrying. There was a massive explosion and I dropped the box and was shocked to see a young woman thrown through a window with her stomach hanging out. Luckily the box, which contained detonators, did not explode or we would have had our legs blown off. I was sickened.

When I got home, I said to my sisters Alice and Phyllis, who had been waiting to see how I had fared : "I'm not going back there again". They laughed at me because they knew I had to go again.

The next day I asked someone what detonators were like. They must have thought I was stupid because someone said: "Those are what you are making now." I nearly fainted.

We had a nice canteen with good food but the cups they served the tea in were usually cracked. Sometimes, we pushed them off the table to break them and get new ones.

German planes came over dropping incendiary bombs and flares to light up the sky for the bomber planes.

I had the job of banging on a big triangle to warn everyone to go into the shelter, then follow them in afterwards.

There were always sheep in the shelters from the fields around the works. In the dark, it wasn't uncommon to sit on a sheep's back and when they ran off, I often found myself covered in sheep muck.

I remember two Irish girls who worked with us came dashing in one night very upset and saying that they had seen two banshees on top of the workshop further down. We came in the night after and that shop had been blown up and a man from Car Bank Street in my home town had been killed and others had been injured.

There was also a ghost of a Madam Weatherby who had been murdered at Oakwood and she had been seen many times walking over the bridge from Group One - Five North.

One of the workers went a bit funny and fixed detonators under the toilet seats. Good job we had been told to lift them up with our feet and not sit on them.

On a lighter note, we had Max Factor officials from Hollywood with new pancake makeup and lipstick telling us how to use it.

It was all free and we were glad of it because we could only normally get face-cream and lipstick now and again.

When we worked nights, some of us had a job to keep awake and someone gave us some pills that the RAF took to keep them awake on bombing missions. I had one and it kept me awake for days afterwards. I kept watch while the others had a nap.

There were Danger Building Inspectors who came round now and again to make sure we were wearing our goggles and we were warned of their approach by workers from other shops who used to whistle a certain tune.

We were issued with new uniforms - white trousers and a coat with a mandarin collar and buttoned down front. We all had to wear caps or turbans.

In the canteen we had concerts at lunchtime with artists from ENSA and sometimes the bosses would dress up and join in. If there was an explosion in the magazine or shops, we all had to go to the canteen for cups of tea and two cigarettes which we had to pay for. The other girls used to argue over my two cigarettes as up to then I didn't smoke.

One day, a young girl came into our shop to sharpen a pencil and she had just gone back when there was such a bang.

Everyone ran to see what it was except me. She had walked in through the door when the explosion occurred. She put her hands on the wall. One of them dropped off along with the fingers of the other hand. She was also blinded. As they wheeled her past on a stretcher, her naturally curly auburn hair was white and straight. Seeing how shocked I was, the group nurse lit a cigarette and made me smoke it, supposedly to calm my nerves. She did the same the following day after another accident.

It was the start of a lifelong habit."

IN THE SPRINGTIME WE ROAMED BI' THE RIBBLE.

This is a sort of allegorical poem where Lancashire's River Ribble becomes the River of Life. It's a bit sad but then life's not all sunshine and flowers. I like to think it has a weirdly optimistic ending. The poem I mean - and Life itself if it comes to that.

In the Springtime we roamed bi the Ribble, arm in arm o-er a carpet o' green
And I picked her a bunch o' breet speedwell, to match booath her bonny blue een.
And we capered like lambs decked i' sunleet, as from't Cuckoo's throeert came't Song o' Joy
An we booath thowt o' nowt but each other - her a wench, me no moor than a boy.

In the Summer we lay bi' the Ribble an' we bathed in Owd Sol's gowden beams
As we nestled and nuzzled together, t'river sparkled and shone like eawr dreams.
Wi eawr yeds on ferget-me-not pillows and eawr hearts up wi't Skylark i' song,
We seed eawr lives stretch eawt afoor us, as far as the river were long.

In the Autumn, we lingered bi't Ribble...then I stayed and she went on ahead.
And the one-o-clocks drifted i' silence, like lost souls i' search o' the dead.
And't River looked cowd and forbiddin' as the swallows sought waarmth o' fresh lands.
Though I thowt I cud stop t'River flowin', I reached eawt but it slipped through me 'ands.

In the Winter we traipsed bi' the Ribble, wi' no Sun but cowd neetfall's mad moan,
And it weren't fer the want of a top-coat that struck me like ice to the bone.
O'erhead came the caw of a carrion crow and I fancied I heeard t'River say:
"Come on lad, it's time theaw were gooin'. I'll wesh aw thi troubles away..."

Neaw i spirit we glide bi' the Ribble. We're the cry o' the Magpie that mocks.

We're the Shadow that follows yer footsteps. We're the Boggart that tugs lovers' locks.

But lay two Red Roses bi't River and eawr blessings upon you we'll bring.

For as long as there's lovers i' Maytime, we'll still roam bi the Ribble i' Spring.

THE PICTURES

The Savoy Cinema in Atherton is now a Snooker Club. In the late 50's and early sixties, it was the main place in town for sheer enjoyment (apart from the Palace Cinema, the Punch Bowl Temperance Bar; the back room of the A1 Chippy and the Zambezi Cafe that is).

On Saturday mornings was the tradition of the Tuppenny Rush when the majority of the town's kids would flock in great excitement to see films specially put on for their enjoyment at a vastly reduced rate.

First of all there would be a cliff-hanger serial starring the inimitable Flash Gordon or Captain Marvo (Can Flash escape the clutches of Ming the Merciless. Tune in next week!!!) Of course he did and we always did.

Then Tom Mix (Blimey, how old must those films have been!) or Lash Laroo or Hopalong Cassidy but our favourite was always Roy Rogers and his trusty steed Trigger who had more brains than the government. How we cheered when Roy decked the baddies. Then it might be a cartoon feature or, joy of joys, the Three Stooges giving us hundreds of different ideas on how to poke each other's eyes out.

One indispensable piece of our armament was the Pea Shooter through which we propelled pigeon peas at the fire extinguishers at the side of the screen during the boring bits - resulting in a very satisfying succession of *"Pings!"* There was a myth that if you hit the screen hard enough, it would burst into flames. Try as we might, we never achieved this ambition.

The was usually accompanied by the frantic bald-headed cinema manager -"Torchy" - running round flashlight in hand in a useless bid to find the culprits and resulting in us shouting to him: *"Put thi' torch out - it's melting me lolly!"*

I remember once being seated on one of the front rows and dropping my peashooter on the floor of the Savoy. Feeling round in the dark, I managed to retrieve it only to find it was dripping wet through. The reason?

The kids in the seats behind had peed on the floor and the slope of the room carried it down to the front. I wiped the peashooter on my sleeve and continued to bombard the fire extinguishers. Antibiotics? Who needed em?

This is in memory of those brilliant times.

SATURDAY COWBOYS

Half past nine on a Saturday morning
Birds are singing and dogs are yawning.
There's a great excitement in the air.
Down along each cobbled street, there comes the sound of tiny feet.
All games are stopped, no time to stand and stare.
Sixpences they're clutching tightly, little eyes all shining brightly.
Happy laughing kids without a care.
As they skip and dance along, they start to sing a special song and
Saturday Cowboys sing it everywhere.

They're singing: Mister Mister why are we waiting, Saturday Cowboys don't like waiting
Come on down and give them doors a push.
We wanna see Lassie and Rin Tin Tin and Charlie Chaplin makes us grin.
Saturday Cowboys love the Saturday rush.

Saturday Cowboys rush to the pictures
Clutching lollies and Dolly Mixtures,
We'll all get there faster if we run.
I've stuck me six gun into me sock and the usherette's in for a nasty shock when a plastic bullet hits her up the bum.

Doors fly open and in they stumble, through the dark they feel and fumble
Every Cowboy's got his favourite seat.

Then they hear the Manager shout:"Oy - make less noise or I'll chuck you out!"
And they don't want to miss their Saturday treat.

Cos they're singing:Mister Mister why are we waiting, Saturday Cowboys don't like waiting
Come on down and give them doors a push.
We wanna see Lassie and Rin Tin Tin and Charlie Chaplin makes us grin.
Saturday Cowboys love the Saturday rush.

Smoking "Woodies" and strikin' matches, Cheering't cavalry and booing th'Apaches Watch Roy Rogers shoot that baddy dead.
I've told me mam that when I'm bigger
I'll buy a horse that's just like Trigger and fill that pesky rentman full of lead.

Suddenly the lights go on
The show is over the West is Won.
No more tomato ketchup to be shed.
Half past twelve on a Saturday morning, birds still singing and dogs still yawning
Saturday Cowboys eyes are tired and red.

But they're singing: Mister Mister why are we waiting, Saturday Cowboys don't like waiting
Dinner's ready so give them doors a push.
Hi Ho Silver away we go,
Galloping down the Road-e-o

Saturday Cowboys have been to the Saturday Rush.
Saturday Cowboys have been to the Saturday Rush.
Saturday Cowboys have been to the Saturday Rush.

Yee ha!!

(Saturday Cowboys was a song written with my old mate Bernard Wrigley, alias the Bolton Bullfrog, to celebrate those happy days...)

ATHERTON - A BRIEF HISTORY

Atherton is a former cotton and coal town in the South West of Lancashire, England. Over 20,000 people live in the town. Sadly, today there are no more mines and no more cotton mills.

Known locally as Bent, its history goes back a surprisingly long way.

Romano-Celtic coins have been found by the side of a stream in a place known as The Valley and in 2003, at Gadbury Fold off Atherleigh Way, archaeologists from Manchester University unearthed evidence of a Roman road and Bronze Age settlement at a multi-million pound business and leisure park development.

The dig at the 300-acre Gibfield Park site in Atherton revealed fragmentary remains of the badly damaged road, which linked Roman forts at Manchester and Wigan and also revealed that mining had been carried out on the site since at least the 14th century.
The archaeologists also discovered evidence of iron smelting in the 16th century.

Assistant county archaeologist for Greater Manchester, Norman Redhead, said: "If this ditch does date to the Bronze Age, it would mean there was human activity in the area 4,000 years ago."

Dig director Peter Connelly, said: "The existence of coal seams very close to the ground surface led the early pioneers of the coal mining industry to the area to carry out small-scale open-cast mining which shows the deep history of the mining tradition in Atherton."

Atherton was at one time also famous for over 600 years for the manufacture of nails, a particular type of which were known as sparables or "sparrow bills" because they were shaped as such. The foundries which replaced the nailworks made machines for the cotton mills early in the Industrial Revolution. A pub on Atherton's Market Street is named The Jolly Nailor.

Other pubs in the street have for some reason best known to their owners been renamed - notably the Wheatsheaf and the King's Head - thus losing a link with Atherton's past.

The principal landowners in the early days were, naturally enough, the Atherton family. Nicholas Atherton was a retainer of the famous John of Gaunt and William and Nicholas Atherton were present at the Battle of Agincourt in 1415.

Chowbent was an area of the town which later became synonymous with Atherton itself. In 1642, during the English Civil War, there was a skirmish between the Royalists and the Roundheads there when the area was attacked by the Earl of Derby and his men. They were repulsed by 3,000 horse and foot and were chased to Lowton Common where several Royalists were killed and 200 taken prisoner. Chowbent nailors were prominent in the fight with their home-made bills and battle axes.

A Market has existed at Atherton for hundreds of years - the first written reference about it being in 1693. Until recent times there was a Market near the Parish Church of St John the Baptist every Friday. Sadly, this petered out around 2003. Another facet of the town lost.

The following is a description of Chowbent from the Lancashire Gazetteer, of Joseph Aston in 1808:

CHOWBENT, 2 ½ miles N.E. of Leigh, 10 miles W.N.W. of Manchester, and 195 miles from London, is in the township of Atherton, and parish of Leigh, under which it has a chapel of ease; patron, Atherton Gwillum, Esq. It has likewise a large dissenting chapel, belonging to a congregation of Presbyterians. This place affords employment for many weavers and nailors, (the later being the original trade of the place) and though it is not a market town, there are many such, which have nothing like the population which Chowbent can boast.

The Parish Church was designed by the renowned architects Messrs Paley and Austin of Lancaster. It is the third such building on the site. A small red-brick Presbyterian chapel was built in 1645 and replaced in 1810 by a larger church. which was demolished 67 years later to be replaced by the present one which took 20 years to complete.

Built in Perpendicular style, it has a Tower 120 feet high and the church itself is 127 feet long and 60 feet wide.

The Tower has a distinct lean due to the consequences of old coal-mining workings.

The church is built of Runcorn stone and it was cleaned in 1973 to reveal beautiful colouring underneath the decades of grime which had accumulated as a result of the outpourings of the many factory chimneys in the area.

Chanters is an old farmhouse which was built in 1678 and now sits somewhat incongruously on a modern housing estate.

The slightly later Alder House also still stands and is a private house after many years use as a clinic. This was built in 1697 by Ralph Astley and his wife Ann. It is thought he was an iron merchant who supplied the nailmakers of Chowbent with the raw material before taking it back as finished work.

According to tradition ,he and his wife were struck by lightning at the same time and are buried in the chapel yard close by.

In 1715, the lives of the Chowbenters became entangled in a very important historical event which affected the rest of English history.

The Parson of Chowbent Chapel - James Wood - gathered together around 80 members of his congregation and marched north to Preston where they were set the task of guarding the ford at Penwortham against the Scottish Jacobite attackers of the 1715 uprising.

Armed mainly with their home-made pikes, bill-hooks and pitchforks, they fought with valour and won the day and formed a decisive part of the battle. The Parson was from that day given the nickname of "General" James Wood. (The General was minister at Chowbent for more than 60 years following his father who had served in the same post for almost 40 years. When he became infirm in his late 80's, the Chowbenters carried this beloved man to the chapel in a sedan chair.)

The brave Chowbenters, for their pains, were ejected from their chapel in 1721 by the landowner "Mad" Richard Atherton whose father had been a firm supporter of King James the Second. They carried on with their worship in barns.

Undaunted, these defiant Lancastrians then built their own chapel on land donated to them a short distance away.

The story of how they did this was written for posterity in "The Story of Chowbent Chapel" by J.J. Wright in 1921.

(Reprints of this fantastic book are now available from Atherton Library at five pounds with profits going to the Chapel. I highly recommend it*)

By a superhuman effort on the part of the congregation, the new chapel was ready for worship in 1722.

The building still stands in Bolton Old Road, Atherton and is a tribute to the craftsmanship and determination of those long-gone Chowbenters. It is now Chowbent Unitarian Chapel and to visit it is like stepping back in time to experience the peace of the chapel and the beauty of its old oak box pews, gallery and triple-decker pulpit. It is a remarkable place.

"General" Jimmy died in 1759 at the considerable age of 87, well loved by his flock.

From an extract of "Philosophical Transactions" for 1775, it is stated that the population of Chowbent (ie. Atherton) in 1772 was 354 males and 606 females.

In 1774, John Wesley preached at Chowbent describing the inhabitants of the area as such: "It was lately a den of lions but they are now all quiet as lambs".

In his Journal he wrote: "Chowbent was once the roughest place in the neighbourhood. But there is not yet the least trace remaining, such is the fruit of the genuine Gospel"

Another visitor to the area was travel writer Dorning Rasbotham in 1787 who said:" Several families have acquired fortunes by making spinning jennies and carding machines which they send into Scotland, Ireland and different parts of the Kingdom. Some of the mechanics do not keep less than 30 journeymen employed in the business".

Mad Richard began his own construction in 1723 – Atherton Hall which was intended to be the new family seat. Built on a grand scale (at a cost then of £63,000) with its own lake and a fancy bridge guarded by stone lions, it was never fully completed as Richard died in 1726. This grand building was demolished in the 1820's although parts of it remain and are lived in to this day.

There was a story that when the bells of Leigh Parish Church struck 12 o'clock on New Year's Eve, the lions used to dive off the bridge into the lake and some people gathered there to witness this!

It is thought that the Hall's grounds hosted the Chowbent Horse Races which took place in the 1770's. On the 26th July 1775, there was a race for the not insubstantial sum of £50.

As the Industrial Revolution took hold, the local handloom weavers were fearful for their livelihoods and in 1812, the Luddites marched from Atherton to nearby Westhoughton to burn down a factory in which new machines driven by steam had been installed.

Three local men and a boy of 14 were caught and hanged at Lancaster Castle. A cart was sent to the castle to retrieve their bodies - it was sent back empty.

In 1777, the population of Chowbent was given as 2,200; in 1801, it was 3,249; in 1811 it numbered 3,894; in 1821, 4,145; in 1831, 4,181. At the beginning of the 20th century, it was over 16,000 due to the development of pits, cotton mills and foundries.
People came from Wales and Ireland to work and be made welcome in the Atherton community, along with miners from the Forest of Dean. Their many descendants live there today.

In 1828, the railway age came early to the town with the opening of the Bolton-Leigh line which passed through Atherton. The world famous George Stephenson himself had built an engine which was brought to the Hulton estate on the outskirts of the town where it was christened "The Lancashire Witch".

Rails were laid and the pulling power of this new mode of transport was demonstrated with 13 wagons carrying the passengers. Later, it was demonstrated how much coal could be carried.

The Lancashire Witch had two furnace flue tubes which joined together at the front into a single chimney. Robert Stephenson also added nozzles in the firegrate through which air was pumped by bellows in the tender. Using this method it was possible to burn coke rather than coal and therefore reduced the amount of smoke produced.

Weighing only seven tons, the Lancashire Witch could pull a load of 40 tons up an incline of 1 in 440 at 8 mph (13 kph).

The cylinders were placed on each side of the boiler that inclined at about forty-five degrees. The pistons drove the front wheels directly. This made her the first locomotive with steel springs on all wheels.

An inventor closer to home was the brilliant Professor Eric Laithwaite - born in Atherton in 1921.

He designed the world's first magnetically levitating train - the MagLev. In an interesting parallel with the Stephenson concept, a mile of track was built and the locomotive was tested but in a short-sighted move, the project was abandoned by the Government.

A former professor of Heavy Engineering at Imperial College, London, he also worked during the war at the Royal Aircraft Establishment at Farnborough on automatic pilots.

At the age of 76, shortly before he died, he was working with America's National Aeronautics and Space Administration - NASA - who had commissioned him to develop a five-mile long track to be tunnelled inside a 10,000 feet high mountain which would hurtle a capsule into space not with conventional rocket propulsion but powered by the professor's beloved linear motors.

Someday, I hope a statue to this very brilliant man will be erected in the town in which he was born. * See story below...

Talking of transport, Atherton was once the headquarters of the L.U.T. - Lancashire United Transport - one of the biggest privately-run bus companies in the country at that time. Behind the office block on Leigh Road, the generating station provided power for the area and also for the trolley buses which ran in the district.

Coal was important to Atherton and brought prosperity to the town. It also brought tragedy when on December 21st, 1910 one of the worst-ever pit disasters in history occurred at the Pretoria

Mine where an explosion killed 333 men, shattering the lives of many a family in the area. A yearly service still takes place to honour the memory of these brave colliers every Christmas.

The partnership of the Fletcher Burrows families dominated the local coal-mining scene.

They adopted a paternalistic attitude towards the people in their employ: building model housing ; a school; a church; a social club; pithead baths and forming mines rescue teams all based at Howe Bridge. Some of the buildings exist today and are well worth going to see.

An Atherton invention saved the life of many coal miners. This was the Butterfly clip invented by Thomas Ormerod which checked the rewinding of a mining cage. It can be seen carved on his tombstone in Atherton Cemetery.

In 1916, the miners from six pits formed the Atherton Collieries Football Club and by 1964\65 they had won the Lancashire Junior Shield six times and produced footballers who have gone on to play with clubs such as Manchester United and Everton.

The "Colls" have a loyal following as do their counterparts in the town - Laburnum Rovers FC. The slope on both pitches has to be seen to be believed.

In 1966, the last of the many coalmines closed down and brought an end to an important part of Atherton's history. Generations of cotton and coal workers were consigned to a footnote of history.

The great cotton mills came and went...and with them the jobs of local people.

Atherton still survives - a proud and defiant Lancastrian town - but touched, as arc a lot of towns, by the troubles of the modern age.

New hope exists for the community as a multi-million regeneration scheme is being put in place which may yet prove its salvation. It remains to be seen. Any employer thinking of relocating or opening up a factory or industrial unit would do well to consider Atherton. You would have a ready-made (and good-humoured) workforce.

But whatever the future brings, Atherton has made its mark on the past and, let us hope, with the help of its young people, it may still have a part to play in tomorrow's world.

Good owd Bent!

BENT - A DERIVATION?

As we know, "Bent" is the local nickname for Atherton.

But where did it come from?

Bent is a type of grass of the genus Agrostis. Bent also is derived from the Old English word "Beonet" which comes from the Old Saxon word "Binet" which means a heath or unenclosed pasture. In other words, when our Saxon forefathers talked about Bent, they probably meant their unenclosed pasture.

"Going up Bent" meant going up into the centre of Atherton - ie, Market Street and not going to Chowbent which is a specific district in Atherton. It is probable that in the past before it became a shopping area, it was unenclosed pastureland.

The "Chow" bit might be a personal suffix as in "Chow's Pasture". after a long-forgotten farmer.

My own personal theory is that it might be a corruption of "Keaw Bent" ie - "Cow Pasture" as locally it is pronounced "Cheawbent". Probably wrong but, then again, as nobody knows for certain, who knows any different..?

DAVE DUTTON

Dave has written many books – most of which are now available on Amazon and other sources.

Along with his legendary Lanky Spoken Here and Lanky Panky, he has a book called How to be a Crafty Cruiser which is full of tips and tricks to get the best out of a cruise holiday.

His Book of Famous Oddballs reveals weird facts about famous people and his Horrors! Book is chock full of grim true tales.

For more information on the author and to find out how to buy his other paperbacks and ebooks, see www.davedutton.co.uk

If you enjoyed the book, please consider leaving a review. Thank you.

Printed in Great Britain
by Amazon